SCIENCE MADE SIMPLE™

# CHEMICAL REACTIONS

PHILIP WOLNY

rosen publishing's
rosen
central®

New York

*To Andre, Justin, and the mad scientists worldwide*

Published in 2011 by The Rosen Publishing Group, Inc.
29 East 21st Street, New York, NY 10010

Copyright © 2011 by The Rosen Publishing Group, Inc.

First Edition

**Library of Congress Cataloging-in-Publication Data**

Wolny, Philip.
Chemical reactions / Philip Wolny. — 1st ed.
    p. cm. — (Science made simple)
Includes bibliographical references and index.
ISBN 978-1-4488-1235-6 (lib. bdg.)
ISBN 978-1-4488-2242-3 (pbk.)
ISBN 978-1-4488-2249-2 (6-pack)
1. Chemical reactions—Juvenile literature. 2. Chemistry—Juvenile literature.
I. Title.
QD501.W794 2011
541'.39—dc22

2010018818

*Manufactured in Malaysia*

CPSIA Compliance Information: Batch #W11YA: For further information, contact Rosen Publishing, New York, New York, at 1-800-237-9932.

**On the cover:** Top: Lighting a candle with a match is one of many everyday activities we perform that involve chemical reactions—in this case, combustion. Bottom: Laboratory scientists preparing and studying the effects of chemical reactions.

# CONTENTS

# INTRODUCTION

**P**ick up any cell phone or smartphone and turn it on. It will light up and start to emit noise. You might ask, "What, exactly, makes this thing run?" The quick answer, of course, is that the phone is battery-powered. The battery is recharged when plugged into a charger that, in turn, is plugged into a wall socket.

But what is happening on a deeper level? Since the discovery of electricity and a way to safely harness it, humans have gained a greater scientific understanding about energy, life processes, and how the two interact. A time traveler from hundreds of years ago might believe that some strange magic powered our phones and other devices. We know better, however.

Still, many of us rarely think about or fully understand the explanations behind how our everyday items, and our world in general, work. We know that a battery provides us with electricity, but how does it do so? The answer to this

Chemical reactions help power the world around us and provide our modern conveniences, such as rechargeable battery-powered cell phones and other mobile devices.

and other questions regarding how and why certain things work, look, or smell the way they do boils down to the subject of this book: chemical reactions.

Though we think of batteries as electrical devices, they actually work as the result of a series of chemical reactions. In other words, the way that chemicals combine and react to each other within the battery is what creates the electrical energy that we draw on to power our various electronic and portable devices. A cell phone battery, while solid in outward appearance, contains several active chemicals inside of it.

When we think of chemical reactions, we often think of things that are far outside of our everyday lives—a lab experiment mixing two bubbling and smoking liquids in a test tube, for example. In this book, we will explore how chemical reactions are working in the world around us and within our own bodies, too.

Baking, for instance, uses heat to help set off a series of chemical reactions among the various ingredients to make bread rise. Cooking alters the chemical composition of many foods. That's why cooked foods and raw ones look and taste different from each other. When bread is eaten, chemicals in the body, called enzymes, help break it down into nutrients that the body can use to sustain its functions. After a meal is finished and it's time to brush our teeth, the ingredients in toothpaste react with water to help scrub the teeth clean. Almost any daily activity can be viewed as a set of chemical reactions. Even when someone is sitting still or sleeping, the air that the person breathes in undergoes chemical changes in the body, helping keep him or her alive.

Chemical reactions really do make the world go round. This book will examine how they impact many areas of our lives and our world: our minds and bodies, technology, work and leisure, and Earth's environment. Human understanding of chemical reactions has also changed over the course of history, and we will investigate exactly how it has done so. We'll also look into how cutting-edge chemical research is improving our everyday lives. Our understanding of chemical reactions can even help us solve some of the world's most urgent problems. This includes those that threaten the very life that chemical reactions help sustain in all living things.

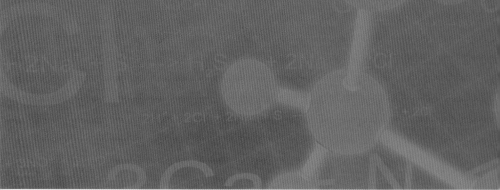

# 1

# WHAT IS A CHEMICAL REACTION?

Before we can examine how chemical reactions work and affect our everyday lives, we first need to define them. What is a chemical reaction? The simple answer is that it is a process or event in which a chemical substance or substances change into a different substance. In a chemical reaction, a change of some kind occurs among the substances involved, which are called reactants. Often, two or more substances interact, creating new substances, or products. These new products have properties or qualities that are different from the original substances.

But let's dig a little deeper: what do we mean by "substance"? A substance is anything with a definite composition. Substances of all kinds exist all around us. For example, things like water, gold,

An overflowing garbage can, once shiny and newly made in a factory, is covered in rust as a result of exposure to moisture in its environment. Many similar chemical reactions occur slowly and are frequently invisible to the naked eye.

salt, acid, or iron are all substances. But they don't just exist on their own, in isolation. Substances are always interacting with each other.

Substances have many qualities that can be used to describe them. Water is a liquid and is clear, for example, while gold is a heavy solid and is shiny and yellowish. Many times, the qualities of substances change when they react with each other. If you've ever seen an old, steel garbage can in the street, you may have noticed that it had parts that turned a reddish color. That's because the iron in the steel reacted with the oxygen in the atmosphere to produce rust. From what was once a shiny, silvery, and strong substance came a dull, reddish, weakened, and crumbly substance: rust.

## CHEMISTRY: THE "CENTRAL SCIENCE"

People tend to think of chemicals as foreign or human-engineered substances that primarily exist in industry, inside science labs, or deposited in machines and weapons. But chemicals are all around us—and within us. Chemicals are found within any solid, liquid, or gas. How chemicals react is a crucial part of biology (the study of living things) and physics (the study of motion and energy). This is why chemistry is sometimes considered "the central science."

## ATOMS, MOLECULES, AND SUBSTANCES

We know what substances are, but there are many different kinds. All matter on Earth—whether air, water, metal, or the living tissue of animals, plants, or humans—is made up of a limited amount of basic parts called elements. At this point, there are only 118 elements that scientists know of, and only about 90 of them occur naturally on the planet.

The basic definition of an element is a substance that cannot be broken down further into a simpler substance by any kind of chemical or physical reaction. (This definition has exceptions, however, including the substances called isotopes.) Water is a substance, for instance, but it can be broken down through certain processes into its two constituent elements: hydrogen and oxygen. Hydrogen and oxygen, however, cannot be

Water is one of the most common substances on Earth, and it is represented here in its basic components—oxygen and hydrogen. One atom of oxygen bonds with two atoms of hydrogen to form a molecule of water. The properties of water differ from those of its two individual components.

broken down any further by conventional means. Water and other substances that are made up of two or more elements are called compounds.

The smallest and most basic unit of an element is the atom. Even one tiny speck of gold contains millions of gold atoms. At a higher level, we have molecules, which are groups of atoms that are bound together by properties of attraction. Molecules can be formed by several atoms of the same element or by combinations of different elements. Thus, one molecule of water contains two atoms of hydrogen and one atom of oxygen. This gives it its chemical formula, $H_2O$. On the other hand, one molecule of oxygen is two atoms of oxygen bound together ($O_2$).

While the atoms of most substances usually cannot be broken down, these tiny components are themselves made up of parts. Electrons, protons, and neutrons are arranged in a specific order and number. This gives elements their specific properties and determines how they will behave in chemical reactions.

When we talk about chemistry, we are basically talking about how chemical bonds are formed. These bonds hold atoms together in molecules and compounds. Atoms exchange or share electrons, which is the real force that "attracts" them. This ease of exchange and attraction is why hydrogen and oxygen so readily form water and why carbon and oxygen combine to form carbon dioxide ($CO_2$).

## PROTONS, ELECTRONS, AND NEUTRONS

All atoms are composed of three components: protons, electrons, and neutrons. These are particles so tiny that they are

# Looking for a Reaction

An easy way to determine if a chemical change has occurred or is occurring is to rely on your senses. Cooking is an example of chemical reactions that we create every day. The smell of cooked, spoiled, or burned food is a clear sign of a chemical reaction having taken place.

Rotten eggs have a very distinctive bad smell, similar to that of a match that has gone out. This is because eggs contain cysteine and methionine. These are amino acids (the building blocks of proteins), which are rich in sulfur. It is the sulfur that gives off that particular smell. This sulfur smell occurs only after carbon dioxide slowly escapes through the egg's shell. The carbon dioxide makes the egg more acidic. Water escapes along with the carbon dioxide, and as the acid and water help decompose the egg, a gas called hydrogen sulfide ($H_2S$) builds up inside. That is why when a rotten egg is cracked open, a bad sulfurous smell is released.

A change in the color of a substance is also a great indicator of a chemical alteration having occurred. Metal turning to rust is one example. The process of rusting is known as oxidation. When metals such as iron and steel are exposed to rain and other moist conditions, the water, which is known as an oxidizing agent, causes corrosion. Oxygen molecules from the air attach to the metal. The iron or steel then becomes corroded and starts to break down into that substance we recognize as rust.

The red streaks and splotches on old bridge supports, pictured here, are a telltale sign that deterioration has occurred due to the corrosion associated with rust. Rust is the result of a chemical reaction in which oxygen and iron react in the presence of moisture.

invisible to us. The atom can be compared to our solar system, with the protons and neutrons in the center, like the sun. The much tinier electrons revolve around this center in paths, or orbits, much like planets. These orbits are also known as electron shells. Protons have a positive electrical charge, while electrons have a negative one. Neutrons have no charge (hence their name, related to the word "neutral").

Each element features atoms containing different numbers of all these particles. An element is defined by its number of protons, which is fixed. The element helium has two protons and two electrons, while hydrogen has one of each, making both of them the lightest of the elements. Other elements have more protons and electrons, making them heavier.

It is the number and combination of protons, electrons, and neutrons that give individual elements—and the many compounds they form—their particular characteristics. These factors also affect which elements will bond more easily with others and which ones will probably never bond unless great force is applied.

A glass saucepan provides a clear view of an everyday process in which a substance is changed from one state of matter to another.

## PHYSICAL REACTIONS

There are many ways that substances can be altered by changing conditions. Two types of changes, or reactions, to a substance are possible: chemical and physical. An example of a physical change is how water changes its state according to

the temperature. In warm weather, a glass of water is in its liquid form. But when the water is put into the freezer, it turns to ice. If water is placed on a lit stove, it will eventually boil and turn into steam, or water vapor. Its physical properties—weight, ability to blend with other substances, and other factors—change as it changes from a solid to a liquid to a gas. But chemically, the substance remains the same: two atoms of hydrogen and one atom of oxygen.

Physical changes can also be brought about by mixing two substances together. For example, if alcohol is added to water, it takes a colder temperature than normal to freeze the combined substances, which we call a mixture. Both water and alcohol keep their individual chemical properties, however, even when mixed together. There has been no change to their chemical composition.

## CHEMICAL REACTIONS: PRODUCING NEW SUBSTANCES

On the other hand, there are instances of everyday reactions in which the chemical nature of the substance or substances involved is indeed altered. A common science lab tool helps illustrate this principle. The Hoffman apparatus uses electricity to split a quantity of water into its constituent parts: hydrogen and oxygen. Each element is collected in a separate part of the apparatus. In this case, water (a substance) experiences a chemical change because its parts (molecules) are broken down into smaller ones (elements). In other words, it is no longer water. The two elements that bond to create water have been broken apart and again exist as separate entities.

Substances can be chemically altered by various factors. Sometimes, a third substance is introduced to two others. Depending on the substances involved, one or even all of them are chemically changed as a result of the interaction. At times, the introduced substance remains the same, while the pre-existing ones are chemically altered. Heat, electricity, and other energy also change the chemical composition of reactants, even if a third substance is not involved.

## MORE THAN MEETS THE EYE

Other physical changes in the qualities of a substance, such as its texture, volume, or appearance, provide hints that a chemical reaction has occurred. A fun experiment involves two eggs. Place one in water and the other in vinegar for twenty-four hours. After a full day, it will be observed that the egg in water has stayed the same. The one in vinegar, however, has lost its shell and feels different. Over time, the vinegar (which is acetic acid) softened and dissolved the calcium carbonate of the eggshell.

However, not all such changes are definitive signs of a chemical change. For instance, when salt is dissolved in water, physical changes occur that cannot be seen. The newly salty water will require a lower temperature than ordinary water to freeze. No change has occurred to either the water or the salt dissolved in it, however. They have mixed but have not changed each other's chemical makeup.

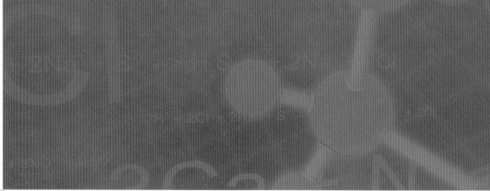

# CHEMICAL REACTIONS IN THE WORLD AROUND US

Chemical reactions make all life possible and powerfully affect the world around us. Indeed, chemical reactions make the world go round. All of the processes that allow life to flourish and survive on Earth are chemical reactions. Whether we are breathing, eating, drinking, walking, or sleeping, chemical reactions occur within our bodies and affect our interaction with the world. The reactions that occur in our environment or are created in medicine, agriculture, food processing, and other industries are also crucial to our survival.

Just like a car needs gasoline, oil, and other substances to operate and remain in good repair, our bodies rely on substances that keep us alive and functioning properly. The most basic of these are

Taking any kind of medication, or ingesting certain foods or other substances, often produces a chemical reaction within the body. Sometimes this reaction is positive and promotes health and healing. Other times, it is harmful.

food, water, and oxygen. At other times, we might need medicine to supply something we're lacking or fight something alien or overabundant in our system. All the chemicals in our body react with the substances we ingest. They can also react very negatively to ones we shouldn't ingest, like toxins. Taking in the good and keeping out the bad assists not only our bodies but also our brains, which are among the most complicated chemical systems in existence.

The study of complex compounds that the element carbon forms with other elements such as oxygen and hydrogen is called organic chemistry. Biochemistry is the study of the chemicals in the human body and in the living tissues of all living creatures, all of which are carbon-based. Biochemists study how the organs and other bodily structures of living things work together. Before investigating the chemical reactions that occur in the human body and power its most basic functions, it is useful to outline the different types of chemical reactions occurring all around us every day.

## ENERGY AND CHEMICAL REACTIONS

A simple way to look at chemical reactions is to describe them in terms of the energy they absorb or release. Think about stretching a rubber band. Because the material resists being pulled, the energy put into stretching it is absorbed as tension by the band. When the rubber band is released, that absorbed energy or tension is also released, allowing the band to shoot far across a room.

In the context of chemical reactions, energy is discussed in terms of the heat added or released by the combining of

Lighting a candle is an example of combustion, one of the most common chemical reactions in the world. If there is not sufficient oxygen in a room or other space, the candle will not light at all and no chemical reaction will take place.

reactants. Endothermic reactions absorb energy from their surroundings and often involve the breaking of the chemical bonds of molecules. Reactions in which bonds are created are exothermic. This means that energy is released into the molecules' surroundings. Remember that "endo-" is a prefix that means inside, while "exo-" means outside.

An example of an endothermic reaction is melting ice. Ice cubes taken out of the freezer absorb heat energy from

## The Incredible Chemical Journey of the Cheeseburger

Perhaps the best example of the chemical reactions associated with eating and digestion is provided by an all-American culinary classic: the cheeseburger.

When you bite into a burger, the parts of your mouth working on chewing it aren't the only ones in motion. Your mouth is producing saliva that, along with your teeth, helps break down the food, both physically and chemically, using substances called enzymes. This starts a process that is completed by digestive acids and enzymes in the stomach and intestines. These eventually reduce the hamburger into simple sugars and proteins that the body can absorb and use to generate energy, promote cell growth, and sustain life.

Hydrochloric acid (HCl) in the stomach kills bacteria in the burger. It also reacts with a substance produced by the stomach called pepsinogen, changing it into pepsin, an enzyme. Pepsin breaks the chemical bonds of the proteins from the beef and cheese. They become peptone and proteose, making them easier to digest. Other digestive enzymes and chemicals in the large and small intestines and liver further extract nutrients from what remains of the food substance, separate them from the waste products that eventually leave the body, and absorb them for the body's energy and cell-building needs.

the warm room. The speed at which the water molecules are moving increases, and the ice slowly turns to water. A typical exothermic reaction is the burning of a candle. Striking a match and lighting a candle causes both the match and the candle to release stored heat through ignition and burning.

# FIVE TYPES OF CHEMICAL REACTIONS

Whether endothermic or exothermic in nature, chemical reactions can be further classified as one of five different types. The five types of chemical reactions are combination reactions (also known as synthesis reactions), decomposition reactions, single displacement reactions, double displacement reactions, and combustion.

## COMBINATION/SYNTHESIS REACTIONS

A combination or synthesis reaction is one in which atoms or molecules combine into something more complex. Combination reactions are usually exothermic and generally involve two elements or compounds combining into another compound. If we know the reactants and their amounts, we can sometimes predict the resulting products.

An example is the way the metal barium combines with fluorine gas, an exothermic reaction. One barium atom and two fluorine atoms react to form one molecule of barium fluoride. This is a transparent crystal that has many optical uses, including in lenses, windows, and high-energy particle detectors. A more everyday combination reaction can be observed when a chemical drain cleaner reacts with water and organic material in a clogged sink or bathtub. The result of the reaction is a breaking down of the organic matter and a clear drain.

## DECOMPOSITION REACTIONS

When matter decomposes, it is broken down into smaller parts. Decomposition is often a very slow process. Just as a beach may erode very slowly over time, a substance may decompose over days, weeks, months, or even centuries. Decomposition is basically the opposite of a combination or synthesis reaction.

This compost heap, a common method of disposing of food and organic refuse and generating rich soil, uses the chemical reaction of decomposition to slowly work its wonders. For many substances, simply exposing them to air or moisture over time is enough to decompose them.

Compounds break down into their component parts, making smaller and simpler molecules. One substance breaks down into two or more separate ones.

One example of decomposition is provided by a can of soda. A solution called carbonic acid ($H_2CO_3$) is often added to soda. This is what gives soda its fizz. Yet once a can of soda has been open for a while, it loses its fizz, or "goes flat." It has gone flat because the carbonic acid has slowly decomposed into carbon dioxide and water.

## SINGLE DISPLACEMENT REACTIONS

A reaction in which one element displaces (replaces) another in a compound is called a single displacement reaction. In such reactions, a metal replaces another metal, or a nonmetal displaces a nonmetal. The majority of single displacement reactions involve a single element and a compound.

## DOUBLE DISPLACEMENT REACTIONS

A double displacement reaction occurs when the anions (negatively charged ions) and cations (positively charged ions) of two different molecules switch places. Two entirely new compounds are formed during this reaction. Imagine that A, B, C, and D represent elements and that we combine two compounds, AB and CD. A and C are cations, and B and D are anions. In a double displacement reaction, the cations and anions of the two compounds switch places. So the cation A forms a bond with the anion D, and the cation C bonds with the anion B. The products of this combination contain the same elements but completely different substances, AD and CB.

This is an automobile's internal combustion engine. While the combustion, or burning, of fossil fuels has been the most common source of energy since the beginning of the Industrial Revolution, humankind is now exploring newer, cleaner sources of power.

## COMBUSTION

One reaction that we hear about most frequently, especially in reference to automobile engines, is combustion. A combustion reaction involves oxygen combining with other compounds to form water and carbon dioxide. This is an exothermic reaction in most cases. Burning certain compounds creates a great deal of heat, which is why combustion is a common way of producing energy to power our vehicles, other machines, and industries.

# HUNGER: A STORY OF CHEMICAL REACTIONS

Eating is one of the most straightforward ways that we can examine how chemicals react within the human body. We cannot only see, taste, and smell food. We can also feel it in our body's digestive system, where chemical reactions are occurring to break down food into nutrients that promote a body's health and sustain life.

Of course, eating is not just mandatory for maintaining life—it also makes us happy. Consuming different foods provides different sensations. This is why people often resort to "comfort food" when they feel sad or anxious. The substances in food trigger certain chemical reactions in our brains. Some nutrients are especially beneficial to brain chemistry. Fish is considered "brain food" because the omega-3s in fish oil are thought to promote better brain functioning. They seem to boost memory, reasoning, and focus. Similarly, caffeine is thought to foster alertness and concentration.

What is really going on when a person is hungry? The mouth may water when someone smells food cooking, especially if it's been a while since the person's last meal. The person might also feel rumbling in his or her stomach and hear it "growling." In all of these instances, the brain, having received the message from the nose, has signaled to the rest of the body that the empty stomach is about to be filled. And various chemicals—digestive acids in the saliva and stomach—have been activated in anticipation of having some food to break down. These cause the watering mouth and rumbling and growling stomach.

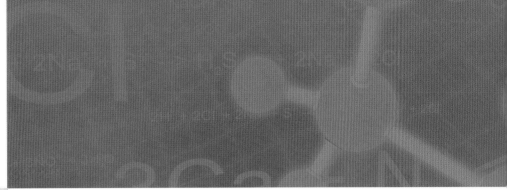

CHAPTER

# 3

# CHEMICAL REACTIONS: A HISTORICAL JOURNEY

Important scientific and technological advances over the last few centuries have provided us with a new and ever-increasing understanding of atoms, elements, and the intricacies of chemical reactions. This quest for chemical knowledge has been a long and enlightening journey, with many different civilizations and brilliant individuals contributing to our growing insight.

## EARTH, AIR, FIRE, AND WATER

Civilizations such as those of ancient Greece, China, Babylonia, and Egypt sought to explain the processes of the physical world. The famous Greek philosopher and thinker Aristotle (born 384 BCE), like earlier Greeks, believed that the universe was composed of four basic building blocks: earth, air, fire, and water. Every bit of matter in the universe was made up of one or a combination of these elements. Ancient belief in these four elements ultimately led to the scientific discovery of the more than one hundred elements of the periodic table that we now take to be the true building blocks of matter.

Similarly, early civilizations made important contributions to the emerging science of chemistry. For example, the Chinese invented gunpowder using their understanding of how sulfur, charcoal, and potassium nitrate reacted in the presence of fire. And the Egyptians devised clever chemical combinations to embalm (preserve from decomposition) the bodies of their dead.

## THE ALCHEMISTS

The efforts of early experimenters who practiced alchemy were extremely important to the study and understanding of chemistry. Alchemists, like today's chemists, tried to create new substances and materials. Many of them were motivated by the belief that they could turn everyday metals into valuable ones, like gold. Some even believed they could create a substance that would grant eternal youth to the person who consumed it. They also sought a "universal solvent," an ideal material that could dissolve any other substance.

Irrational and far-fetched alchemical beliefs were common among different cultures well into the seventeenth and eighteenth centuries. Some more talented and insightful alchemists dug deeper, however, and were genuinely scientifically

This oil painting from 1570, called *The Alchemist's Studio*, depicts the early innovators of chemistry, called alchemists. Alchemists paved the way for the chemical revolution of the modern era.

curious. At the same time, medieval scholars helped preserve the vast learning of the classical world that had nearly disappeared with the fall of the Roman Empire and the barbarian invasions across Europe. The rediscovery and reintroduction of ancient classical texts in the late Middle Ages helped spark the Renaissance, a period of great cultural and scientific progress. Newer scientific theories were flowering, and soon an exciting new age of chemical discoveries was underway.

## THE FATHER OF MODERN CHEMISTRY

Many great innovators of the Renaissance were simultaneously interested in the fine arts, language, classical texts, and science. A broad range of learning and accomplishments was common among the great thinkers, artists, and scientists of the day. This phenomenon resulted in the expression "Renaissance man," which we use today to describe someone with well-rounded skills and interests.

Though born in the later Age of Reason of the eighteenth century, Antoine Lavoisier (1743–1794) was a Renaissance man. Today, he is frequently referred to as the "father of modern chemistry." Lavoisier revolutionized the field when he theorized that, instead of the four elements of antiquity, an element could more properly be defined as anything that could not be broken down into smaller parts. This opened the door to the scientific investigations that resulted in the discovery of more than a hundred elements The process continues today as more elements continue to be discovered periodically. Perhaps Lavoisier's most important contributions to chemistry, however, were his experiments with combustion, or burning.

This color illustration from a *c.* 1900 French textbook depicts Antoine Lavoisier, a well-rounded thinker and pioneer known as the father of modern chemistry.

The ancients believed that fire was a kind of spirit, called phlogiston, that escaped burning objects. Lavoisier performed experiments comparing diamonds that were burned in the open air versus diamonds burned within a special container. He also tested burning candles under various conditions. All of these experiments led him to the conclusion that oxygen was necessary for combustion.

Lavoisier's discoveries showed that earlier theories concerning fire and combustion were incorrect. When some metals burned, for example, they became heavier. The added presence of oxygen during combustion explained this extra weight. It also explained why some metals, when decomposing, released oxygen. Lavoisier's ideas on combustion sparked what some have called the "Chemical Revolution."

## DMITRI MENDELEYEV: THE PERIODIC TABLE

In nearly every chemistry lab or classroom hangs a chart that lists all of the known elements in a very specific order. This is the famous periodic table of the elements. It was first developed by the Russian chemist Dmitri Mendeleyev (1834–1907) as part of a chemistry textbook for students.

His chart was important for many reasons. It was not merely a list of the known elements of the time; it also gave scientists an important new way of thinking about how elements interacted with and related to each other. The periodic table's name comes from the organization of the elements into different "periods."

Mendeleyev used separate cards listing each element. Sorting through them, he began to notice the relationships among their weights and other characteristics. On his table, he arranged the elements from lightest to heaviest (moving left to right). Elements with similar properties aligned with each other in vertical rows. Elements in the modern periodic table are arranged into metal, metalloid, and nonmetal groups. This organization gives users of the periodic table a simple and efficient way to quickly grasp how reactive any given element is compared to the others.

## THE MARCH OF PROGRESS

Numerous scientists further developed the science of chemistry in the years after Lavoisier and his peers made their advances. In 1803, the Quaker John Dalton (1766–1844) proposed his atomic theory that all matter was composed of tiny particles that could not be broken down any further.

Dalton believed that any given atom of gold was identical to any and all other atoms of gold, but that atoms of a particular element would be different from the atoms of other elements.

The atoms of different elements can be distinguished from each other by their differing atomic weights. Dalton further theorized that an atom of one element can combine with atoms of other elements to form chemical compounds, but atoms cannot be broken down into smaller units.

Chemical reactions may reconfigure atoms, breaking down compounds into their separate elements or creating new compounds. But they can't destroy atoms, break them into smaller particles, or create new atoms. Atoms combine to form compounds—such as when hydrogen and nitrogen form ammonia—and this compound will always have the same relative number of types of atoms. Only the combinations of atoms change in a chemical reaction, not the atoms themselves.

While not all of Dalton's ideas were accurate, they opened doors to other scientists who would refine his work. Other vital contributions came from Jons Jacob (J. J.) Berzelius (1779–1848) of Sweden. He furthered Dalton's ideas that atoms combine in predictable proportions in compounds. In

English chemist John Dalton is shown here in an engraving from 1814, based on an original oil painting.

doing so, Berzelius also discovered and isolated many elements, such as selenium (Se) and silicon (Si). Predicting the ways that reactants behaved was a huge advance for chemistry.

## The Atomic Age and Beyond

Building on the ideas of Dalton and others, scientists working around the turn of the twentieth century ushered in the ideas that eventually made possible what we now call the "Atomic Age." Several innovators were important in this new age of discovery.

Antoine Henri Becquerel (1852–1908), who performed experiments on fluorescence and phosphorescence, discovered that bits of uranium left in a drawer with photographic plates would actually begin to expose those plates like light would. This was an important discovery because Becquerel had

## Chemists Fighting Disease

Somewhat more famous than Dalton and Berzelius was Louis Pasteur (1822–1895), the Frenchman who proposed that diseases could be caused by infectous bacteria. Equipped with newer instruments like microscopes, Pasteur and his peers had an advantage over their predecessors.

Pasteur developed the concept of immunochemistry. The process he developed that bears his name, pasteurization, remains an important process for sterilizing wine and milk to prevent disease. Other chemists also helped fight disease, including Joseph Lister (1827–1912), who pushed for the use of antiseptics in surgery. These are chemicals that would keep hospital and surgical environments free of disease. You may be familiar with the product that bears his name, Listerine, a well-known antiseptic mouthwash.

assumed that the photo development process could not happen without an external energy source. But the uranium had generated its own energy somehow.

## THE CURIES AND RADIOACTIVITY

Two other scientists who worked in Becquerel's lab, Marie Curie (1867–1934) and Pierre Curie (1859–1906), took his work to the next level. Pierre discovered that uranium and other elements released energy, or emanations, that made air conduct electricity. The Curies' continuing experiments with types, or ores, of uranium led them to coin the term "radio-active." Initially, they incorrectly believed that radioactivity was somehow added to the uranium, rather than already being present or pre-existing within the uranium.

Eventually, the Curies made measurements of various radioactive elements. They were among the first to measure rates of radiation and discover that radioactivity decreased predictably over time. Perhaps Marie Curie's greatest contribution to the emerging

French physicians Marie and Pierre Curie, Nobel Prize winners in both 1903 and 1911, are shown working in their laboratory.

study of radioactivity was her discovery that radioactivity was a characteristic of particular elements, rather than an outside or unknown force existing within or alongside them.

## RUTHERFORD: THE STRUCTURE OF THE ATOM

New Zealander Ernest Rutherford (1871–1937) went even further when he sought to describe the actual structure of the atom itself. By bombarding gold foil with tiny radioactive particles, he discovered that while some of the particles bounced back, most passed through the foil. This experiment showed that matter was mostly made up of empty space, rather than being completely solid.

Rutherford would later develop the concept of the atom resembling a planetary system with protons, neutrons, and electrons "orbiting" the central nucleus. He also showed how radioactive elements decay. Rutherford's pioneering work allowed future scientists to "split" the atom, releasing tremendous amounts of nuclear energy that could be used for activities both destructive (bombs) and constructive (power plants).

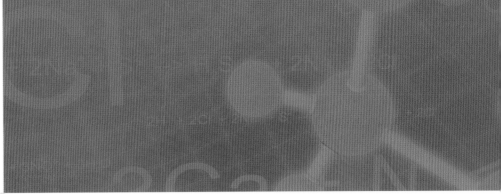

# CHEMISTRY TO THE RESCUE!

We are living in a high-tech age, yet the world is still confronted by many stubborn problems. One of the most effective ways that we can fight or solve them is by drawing upon all of the knowledge that we have inherited, built upon, and advanced. In the "central science," the discoveries and advances made by chemists have impacted human industry, medicine, agriculture, work, and play. Indeed, chemistry has influenced—and, in most cases, greatly improved—most aspects of human life.

Twenty-first-century chemists are using cutting-edge techniques to develop methods for fighting disease, creating new prescription drugs, and growing food (and developing new types of food). Many ambitious scientists also hope that continued research into chemical reactions will help us develop new, green energy sources to replace oil, gas, and coal. This may even help slow down climate change, a major problem facing the world today.

## FIGHTING DISEASES

Centuries ago, it was hard to stop the spread of disease. That's because both scientists and laypeople alike did not really understand how diseases moved among populations. Later, preventing disease using antiseptic and antibacterial techniques like Pasteur's and Lister's saved many lives. But what are scientists doing these days, especially when it comes to chemical reactions, to fight disease?

Viruses are microscopic organisms that invade bodily tissues, often causing illness and disease. They use the genetic code of the cells that they invade against the host because they can't survive on their own. A flu virus can be deadly because it uses a cell's organic structures to manufacture even more copies of itself. If enough are created and they overwhelm the body's immune defense, the host can die. Viruses range from the relatively mild—like the cold virus—to the more dangerous and potentially deadly, like chickenpox (especially when contracted as an adult), smallpox, Ebola, and HIV. Any virus, no matter how mild in ordinary circumstances, can become dangerous to someone with a weakened immune system.

Vaccines work because they trick the human body into creating the biochemical tools needed to fight viruses. Usually, vaccines use part of the genetic code of a virus or something that closely replicates it to encourage the body's natural defenses to

H1N1 vaccinations are administered at St. Barnabas Presbyterian Church in Dallas, Texas. Chemists are studying ways to use chemical reactions to make vaccines longer-lasting and easier to store and transport.

learn how to fight off the actual virus. The body's immune system responds to a vaccine by creating strong defenses against the virus in question. Governments and health organizations create vast amounts of vaccine doses to help protect people from disease outbreaks. However, vaccines are vulnerable to the environment. They are often stored frozen to protect them from heat, which tends to cause chemical decomposition. Because vaccines are often expensive to begin with, transporting them to where they are most needed while keeping them frozen can be very costly, especially for poorer nations.

As reported by the BBC in February 2010, Oxford University scientists recently revealed the results of experiments in which they used special membranes to dry pieces of viruses used in vaccines. This kept them stable even in high temperatures, which would normally kill them within weeks. The scientists noted that the addition of certain sugars to the vaccines as they were slowly dried prevented a decomposition reaction from occurring.

These new techniques could allow vaccination programs to become far more mobile and far less expensive. Dr. Matt Cottingham told the BBC, "Without the need for refrigeration, you could even picture someone with a backpack taking vaccine doses on a bike into remote villages."

## BUILDING BETTER PLANTS

The chemical reactions that occur within crops, livestock (farm animals), and raw and processed foods have been closely

## Organic Chemists Trick the Invading Enemy

Some chemists hope to better treat or prevent illness while creating new foods. Many dangerous organisms latch onto human cells at special sites called receptors. Cold viruses (there are more than two hundred different kinds) could be thwarted by foods engineered to be rich in compounds that lock into such chemical receptors. These compounds would block the entry of viruses and other microbes.

Scientists are also exploring techniques using foods and drugs that have their own receptors so similar to those in human cells that they trick invading microbes. The alien, disease-causing organism could attach to the receptors in the food instead of those in healthy body cells. Through the normal digestive process, these viruses would then exit the body safely.

analyzed by agricultural and food scientists. They also examine the reactions among foods, preservatives, additives, and other substances. Special growing techniques, including genetic engineering, have changed the way we think about food production in the modern era, increasing both yield and resistance to disease or pests.

One of the most basic chemical reactions on Earth is photosynthesis. This is the process in which plants take in light, air, and nutrients to survive. Plants take water and carbon dioxide from the atmosphere and change them into glucose, a

A mechanical cotton picker harvests cotton in a field near Clarksdale, Mississippi. The study of chemical reactions in plant biology has led to the creation of genetically modified crops in recent years.

common sugar. They then release oxygen as a waste product. The glucose becomes starch, which provides the plant with the chemical energy needed for life.

Using this knowledge of photosynthesis, botanists and organic chemists have been working to speed up and improve the process in certain crops and plants. For the last decade, some genetic engineers have concentrated on the enzyme RuBisCO. Short for ribulose-1,5-bisphosphate carboxylase/oxygenase, this enzyme aids the conversion of carbon dioxide during photosynthesis. If plants could be engineered to make better use of this enzyme, they could grow faster and larger.

## THE CHEMISTRY OF FOOD

From the fields where we grow and harvest new types of crops, to the places we buy them, to our dinner tables, chemical reactions are continuously occurring—and being altered by food chemists. These chemists play a huge role in the processing of the items found on supermarket shelves. Slight changes in ingredients and additives can change the taste, nutritional value, and even the texture of food in major ways.

Food chemists also study how the processing, heating, canning, freezing, and packaging of foods affect them. They examine how long foods stay fresh, how they smell, and their mineral and vitamin content. There is a good chance that a favorite cereal, baked snack, or other item, for example, was experimented on to determine how well the chemical reactions that occurred while baking or processing it contributed to a tasty finished product.

# CHEMICAL REACTIONS AND "GREEN CHEMISTRY"

Many chemical researchers and other scientists are developing new chemical techniques, substances, and products while also trying to be environmentally conscious and sustainable. That is, they want to design and use chemicals that pose the least possible danger to the health of the environment and the living things that come into contact with them. This new "green chemistry," or sustainable chemistry, aims to make chemical use in industry, medicine, and other fields safer. There is even hope that chemicals can be used to help clean up the messes that we have made in the past.

Reporting on the efforts of research chemists at McGill University, in Montreal, Canada, *McGill News* discussed the green chemistry movement in a 2005 article. A leader in the field, chemistry professor Tak-Hang Chan, told *McGill News*, "Green chemistry is a new science which will bring all the benefits of chemistry without the costs to the environment."

The movement also challenges scientists to think more deeply about chemical reactions. According to *McGill News*, we are asked to imagine a reaction in which A and B are the reactants, while C and D are the products of the chemical reaction. Often, C is a useful product, while D is waste of some kind, possibly even toxic. Green chemistry pushes chemists to develop reactions in which A and B yield only C, or result in a C and D that are both useful products. In essence, this would be a chemical reaction that produces no waste product, whether toxic or nontoxic.

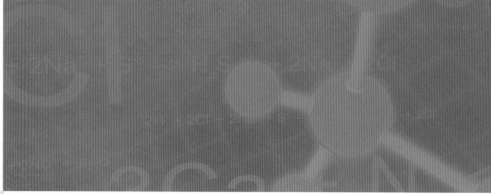

# CLEANER, GREENER CHEMICAL REACTIONS

Chemical reactions are not only happening in the atmosphere. We are also creating them with our cars, factories, and other machines. It is the pollution from human activity that has created the conditions that foster global warming and climate change. But it could also be our improved understanding of how all of these things work together that lets us tackle the problem. In effect, chemistry may save the world.

## THIS GREENHOUSE EARTH

Most scientists agree on the basic problem: our cars, factories, agriculture, and other human activities all require energy, most of which is provided by fossil fuels. Fossil fuels are the carbon-rich remains

Cattle await shipping while padlocked on a feedlot. Raising large amounts of livestock, like cattle, produces large amounts of methane, mainly as a result of digestive processes. Methane is one of the greenhouse gases in the atmosphere whose levels are increasing dramatically, resulting in global warming and climate change.

of ancient plant and animal life. Carbon is one of the essential elements that make life on Earth possible. But when combustion occurs—when coal or oil is burned to generate energy—the carbon locked in the fossil fuels is released and bonds with oxygen. It then enters the atmosphere as carbon dioxide ($CO_2$).

Carbon dioxide is part of the natural cycle of life. Humans and animals exhale carbon dioxide, which plants absorb. The plants then release oxygen, which humans and animals breathe in, and the cycle repeats itself. Carbon dioxide and other so-called greenhouse gases are what make life on Earth possible. They trap heat in the atmosphere, preventing heat loss that would make the planet far too frigid to support most life-forms.

Human activity, however, has pumped far greater amounts of carbon dioxide and other greenhouse gases into the atmosphere than was typical before the Industrial Revolution. The U.S. Environmental Protection Agency (EPA) estimates that $CO_2$ concentrations in the atmosphere are 35 percent higher than they were before the 1700s, an increase that continues to grow every year. The result is a sharp and rapid warming of the atmosphere and surface temperatures that is actually beginning to change climates around the world.

## THE MAIN CULPRIT: THE INTERNAL COMBUSTION ENGINE

One of the largest sources of human-generated greenhouse gases has been the automobile. Cars and trucks are powered by internal combustion engines, which, in turn, are powered by gasoline derived from oil. The basic combustion process occurs within a closed space (the engine), thus it is "internal." A spark ignites the fuel—gasoline rich with hydrocarbons—that combines with oxygen and causes an explosion. This explosion pushes pistons, and the vehicle is powered into motion.

But this process, multiplied by the ignition and operation of billions of motor vehicles daily, is far from clean. In fact, vehicles that rely upon internal combustion engines emit tremendous amounts of pollution, chiefly in the form of the greenhouse gases carbon dioxide, carbon monoxide, and nitrogen oxide.

# Methane-Eating Microbes!

To combat global warming and counteract the effects of deforestation and ocean acidification, we need all the help we can get. Understanding the chemical reactions associated with even the smallest organisms can help us put them to use for the benefit of the whole planet.

In November 2007, the world first heard about *Acidimethylosilex fumarolicum*, a specialized bacterium living in volcanic areas of Earth's surface. This bacterium had adapted in such a way that it can consume methane, one of the three most abundant greenhouse gases in the atmosphere. This discovery gave some chemists the idea to grow such organisms for use in large-scale efforts to reduce atmospheric methane, thus reducing its impact on ongoing and future climate change patterns.

Isoprene, a gas important to the production of rubber and vitamins, provides another interesting example of the complex roles that bacteria can play in controlling greenhouse gases. Plants and algae release isoprene, which reacts with certain molecules to make ozone, another greenhouse gas. Isoprene's presence also helps keep methane in the atmosphere for a longer time before dissipating.

Experiments performed by scientist Dr. Terry McGenity have shown how certain bacteria produced by algae in coastal areas are able to consume isoprene before it even enters the atmosphere. McGenity and his colleagues also noted how these bacteria may break down alkanes, an important compound in crude (unprocessed) oil. This means that the bacteria could be used to help clean up oil spills in ocean waters.

## CLEANING UP COAL

Studying chemical reactions has made scientists and other observers hopeful that we can move away from a reliance on fossil fuels (oil, gas, and coal) to cleaner renewable energy sources. Many of the principles behind some of these solutions are, at first glance, quite simple. Hydrogen fuel cells, biofuels, carbon capture, and clean coal technologies are just some of the new ideas being developed by chemists in the energy industry.

Belching and billowing smokestacks are an unpleasant reminder of what has been sacrificed to meet the world's energy needs. Yet by studying the chemical reactions associated with energy extraction and creation, humans may strike upon practical new sources of clean and efficient renewable power.

Besides oil and gas, coal is perhaps one of the United States' greatest energy sources and accounts for much of the nation's electricity. Yet coal releases huge amounts of both carbon and sulfur into the atmosphere, along with other harmful particulates and gases. So-called acid rain is one common environmental hazard associated with the emissions from coal-powered plants.

Crushing coal into small pieces and literally washing it is one technique that is being explored to reduce emissions. For coal that is chemically bonded with sulfur, called organic sulfur, this cleaning process is not enough. All coal-powered plants built after 1978 are required to install flue gas desulfurization units. More commonly known as scrubbers, these systems can remove some of the particulates and gases that would otherwise be emitted into the atmosphere via smokestack exhaust. Crushed limestone rock is used to extract sulfur from the smoke being emitted. Other processes, which are far more costly, use chemicals to separate the bonds forged between coal and sulfur molecules. Scientists are currently working on ways to make all of these pollution control methods less expensive and more efficient.

## CARS IN A NEW ENERGY AGE

Many of the gases emitted through the burning of fossil fuels and the use of internal combustion engines heat up and/or pollute the atmosphere. For this reason, many people believe that new and cleaner forms of energy are the key to helping humanity avoid environmental catastrophe in the twenty-first century.

New fuels, such as crop-based ethanol, might help. A recent study at the Rochester Institute of Technology, based in Rochester, New York, tested the new E20 fuel, a blend of 20 percent ethanol with 80 percent gasoline. The study found that E20 performs just as well in tests as the 10 percent ethanol fuels already in common use. The 20 percent solution also boasts greater reductions in hydrocarbon and carbon monoxide emissions. The EPA has declared that the amount of renewable fuel in use in the United States must increase from 9 billion gallons (34 billion liters) in 2008 to 36 billion gallons (136 billion liters) in 2022.

Fuel-efficient cars like hybrids, which rely on both electric and gas power, have become enormously popular. Their continued acceptance by the driving public will be of crucial importance in a world where fossil fuels are becoming rarer, more expensive, more controversial, and less popular. Driving smaller cars, using them more efficiently, and trying to use public transportation more frequently will also help break dependence on fossil fuels and reduce harmful greenhouse emissions and air pollution.

## LOSING AN IMPORTANT CARBON SINK

Carbon dioxide levels are rising. Yet because of deforestation and development, we are slowly losing the forests and plant life that help cycle this gas out of the atmosphere. In addition, our oceans play an important role in the climate change cycle, serving as a "carbon sink" that removes carbon dioxide from the atmosphere. Yet, due to global warming, they, too, are becoming less efficient as this task.

Oceans absorb more carbon dioxide than the world's trees and plants

Farmers in China plant trees on a hillside in hopes that they'll prevent erosion, drought, and desertification.

do. They absorb almost one-third of all carbon dioxide that humans release into the air. They act as a sort of carbon dioxide sponge to such a degree that they have probably slowed the still-rapid rate of climate change. But scientists fear that such carbon sinks are becoming overwhelmed. As more carbon dioxide collects in the oceans, the waters become more acidic. This kills off the phytoplankton that is the major consumer of carbon (and an important food source for marine life).

## THE MOST IMPORTANT REACTION

Our growing body of chemical and other scientific knowledge has given us the tools to recognize what is happening around us and why. Yet the only way that we can safeguard the planet and the life it sustains is to use this knowledge intelligently, creatively, and effectively. This means not just waiting for chemists and other scientists to arrive at solutions or remedies for climate change and other problems in our environment. Instead, we must also make changes to our own lifestyles and push for change in society. Science has allowed us to identify the problems facing us. The rest is up to us as individuals, communities, and nations.

A growing understanding of chemical reactions and the application of this knowledge to a wide range of fields will remain a driving force in the way we see our world and the way we adapt to a changing environment. Human manipulation of chemical reactions has in some ways brought us closer to environmental catastrophe, but it can also bring us back from the brink. Intelligent use of chemistry may just save our planet and the life it supports, including our own.

**atom** The smallest particle of matter that has the characteristics of a particular element.

**chemical bond** A strong attraction between two or more atoms.

**chemical reaction** A process by which some chemicals, called reactants, produce an entirely new substance. The original substance has changed on the molecular level and is a different substance altogether.

**combustion** A chemical reaction that produces heat and light, especially with the addition of oxygen; burning.

**compound** Atoms of two or more types sharing a chemical bond.

**electron** One of the subatomic particles that composes an atom; an electron carries a negative electric charge.

**electron shell** The path, or orbit, of an electron around the nucleus of an atom.

**element** A substance formed of atoms of only one type; the basic chemical building block of matter.

**endothermic** Refers to chemical reactions that absorb heat.

**exothermic** Refers to chemical reactions that release heat.

green chemistry  A movement among chemists to approach their field in a way that minimizes hazardous chemical waste and harm to the environment.

mixture  Two or more compounds (or atoms) that are mixed together but not bonded chemically.

molecule  Two or more atoms, either of the same element or different ones, that are joined together chemically.

neutron  One of the subatomic particles that composes the nucleus of an atom; a neutron carries no electric charge.

nucleus  The center of any atom, composed of protons and neutrons.

periodic table  A chart that lists all of the known chemical elements, arranged into groups, or "periods," to show similarities between and among them.

physical reaction  A change that occurs physically to a substance or substances; the state of the substance's matter and energy may change, but this does not result in a new substance.

product  The end result of a chemical reaction.

proton  One of the subatomic particles that composes the nucleus of an atom; a proton carries a positive electric charge.

reactant  A substance that is consumed in the course of a chemical reaction.

solution  A mixture formed when a substance or chemical is dissolved in a liquid.

### American Chemical Society (ACS)

1155 Sixteenth Street NW
Washington, DC 20036
(800) 227-5558
Web site: http://www.acs.org
The ACS is a professional and scholarly organization
of chemists that puts out dozens of publications,
holds conferences, and promotes chemistry in
general.

### Chemical Heritage Foundation

315 Chestnut Street
Philadelphia, PA 19106
(215) 925-2222
Web site: http://www.chemheritage.org
The Chemical Heritage Foundation is an independent
nonprofit organization whose goal is to foster
knowledge about chemistry and its contributions
with public outreach, a chemical library, and other
efforts.

### Chemical Institute of Canada (CIC)

130 Slater Street, Suite 550
Ottawa, ON K1P 6E2
Canada
(888) 542-2242
Web site: http://www.chemistry.ca

The CIC is an umbrella group of three organizations—the Canadian Society for Chemistry, the Canadian Society for Chemical Engineering, and the Canadian Society for Chemical Technology.

### Massachusetts Institute of Technology (MIT)

Department of Chemistry
77 Massachusetts Avenue
Cambridge, MA 02139-4307
(617) 253-1803
Web site: http://web.mit.edu
MIT is one of the most respected and prestigious universities in the world, specializing in science and technology, with a well-known chemistry department.

### National Science Foundation (NSF)

4201 Wilson Boulevard
Arlington, VA 22230
(800) 877-8339
Web site: http://www.nsf.gov
The NSF provides up to 20 percent of all federally distributed money to support science research at colleges and universities nationwide.

### University of Toronto

Department of Chemistry
80 St. George Street
Toronto, ON M5S 3H6
Canada
(416) 978-3564

Web site: http://www.chem.utoronto.ca
The University of Toronto's chemistry department is one of
    Canada's top centers for chemical research.

**U.S. Environmental Protection Agency (EPA)**
Green Chemistry Program
Industrial Chemistry Branch
1200 Pennsylvania Avenue NW
Mail Code 7406M
Washington, DC 20460
(202) 564-8740
Web site: http://www.epa.gov/greenchemistry
The EPA is the federal government agency in charge of pro-
    tecting U.S. natural and environmental resources and the
    health of the American people through enforcement and
    promotion of national standards.

# WEB SITES

Due to the changing nature of Internet links, Rosen Publishing
has developed an online list of Web sites related to the subject
of this book. This site is updated regularly. Please use this link
to access the list:

http://www.rosenlinks.com/sms/chem

Baldwin, Carol. *Mixtures, Compounds, and Solutions* (Material Matters). Portsmouth, NH: Heinemann, 2005.

Brent, Lynette. *Chemical Changes* (Why Chemistry Matters). New York, NY: Crabtree Publishing Company, 2008.

Cooper, Sharon Katz. *The Periodic Table: Mapping the Elements* (Exploring Science). Mankato, MN: Compass Point Books, 2007.

Ham, Becky. *The Periodic Table* (Essential Chemistry). New York, NY: Chelsea House, 2008.

Karpelenia, Jenny. *Chemical Reactions* (Reading Essentials in Science–Physical Science). Logan, IA: Perfection Learning, 2005.

Karpelenia, Jenny. *Physical and Chemical Properties and Changes* (Reading Essentials in Science). Logan, IA: Perfection Learning, 2007.

Kirchner, Renee. *Chemical Reactions* (KidHaven Science Library). Farmington Hills, MI: KidHaven Press, 2006.

Lew, Kristi. *Chemical Reaction*s. New York, NY: Chelsea House, 2008.

Manning, Phillip. *Chemical Bonds* (Essential Chemistry). New York, NY: Chelsea House, 2009.

Saunders, Nigel. *Exploring Chemical Reactions* (Exploring Physical Science). New York, NY: Rosen Publishing Group, 2007.

Slade, Suzanne. *Atoms and Chemical Reactions* (Library of Physical Science). New York, NY: PowerKids Press, 2007.

Solway, Andrew. *Fossil Fuels* (Energy for the Future and Global Warming). Strongsville, OH: Gareth Stevens Publishing, 2007.

Solway, Andrew. *From Gunpowder to Laser Chemistry: Discovering Chemical Reactions* (Chain Reactions). Portsmouth, NH: Heinemann, 2008.

Stille, Darlene R. *Nature Interrupted: The Science of Environmental Chain Reactions* (Headline Science). Mankato, MN: Compass Point Books, 2008.

Thomas, Isabel. *Fireworks!: Chemical Reactions* (Raintree Fusion: Physical Science). Portsmouth, NH: Heinemann, 2007.

Walker, Denise. *Chemical Reactions* (Core Chemistry). Mankato, MN: Smart Apple Media, 2007.

# BIBLIOGRAPHY

Appenzeller, Tim. "The Case of the Missing Carbon." *National Geographic*, September 2004. Retrieved February 2010 (http://ngm.nationalgeographic.com/ngm/0402/feature5/online_extra.html).

Bryner, Jeanna. "Methane-Eating Bacteria Could Save the World." FOX News, LiveScience, November 14, 2007. Retrieved February 2010 (http://www.foxnews.com/story/0,2933,311742,00.html).

Dreaper, Jane. "Fridge-free Vaccine Hopes Raised." BBC News, February 18, 2010. Retrieved March 2010 (http://news.bbc.co.uk/2/hi/health/8520825.stm).

Evernden, Margery. *The Experimenters: Twelve Great Chemists*. Greensboro, SC: Avisson Press, 2001.

Loeschnig, Louis V. *Chemistry Experiments* (No-Sweat Science). New York, NY: Sterling Publishing, 1994.

Madrigal, Alexis. "New Material Could Drop Cost of Carbon Capture." Wired.com, February 29, 2008. Retrieved March 2010 (http://www.wired.com/wiredscience/2008/02/new-material-co).

Mann, Charles C. "Future Food: Bioengineering, Genetic Engineers Aim to Soup Up Crop Photosynthesis." *Science*, No. 15, January 15, 1999. Retrieved February 2010 (http://www.sciencemag.org/cgi/content/short/283/5400/314).

McDonagh, Patrick. "The Green Chemistry Revolution." *McGill News*, 2005. Retrieved March 2010 (http://www.mcgill.ca/news/2005/summer/green).

Newton, David E. *Chemical Elements*. Florence, KY: Gale Cengage, 1998.

O'Meara, Neil. "The Big Picture of Tiny Viruses." *Wisconsin Engineer Magazine*, September 2009. Retrieved March 2010 (http://www.wisconsinengineer.com/webcgi-bin/archivearticle.php?article=sep09virus).

Physorg.com. "E20 Fuel Reduces Carbon Monoxide and Hydrocarbon Emissions in Automobiles." March 29, 2010. Retrieved April 2010 (http://www.physorg.com/news189079957.html).

Stwertka, Albert. *A Guide to the Elements*. 2nd ed. New York, NY: Oxford University Press, 2002.

U.S. Department of Energy. "Cleaning Up Coal: The Clean Coal Technology Program." Retrieved March 2010 (http://fossil.energy.gov/education/energylessons/coal/coal_cct2.html).

U.S. Environmental Protection Agency. "Greenhouse Gas Emissions." Retrieved March 2010 (http://www.epa.gov/climatechange/emissions).

Wiker, Benjamin, and Jeanne Bendick. *The Mystery of the Periodic Table* (Living History Library). Bathgate, ND: Bethlehem Books, 2003.

Zannos, Susan. *Dmitri Mendeleyev and the Periodic Table* (Uncharted, Unexplored, and Unexplained). Hockessin, DE: Mitchell Lane Publishers, 2004.

# INDEX

## ABOUT THE AUTHOR

Philip Wolny is a writer and editor raised in New York. The bulk of his surprisingly rigorous science instruction occurred at Stuyvesant High School, one of the premier science high schools in the United States.

## PHOTO CREDITS

Designer: Sam Zavieh; Photo Researcher: Marty Levick